I Learned How to Fly in the Rain

A Story of Resilience

La'Quanna Lampley

I LEARNED HOW TO FLY IN THE RAIN
Copyright © 2022 by La'Quanna Lampley

Published by Cornerstone Publishing
www.thecornerstonepublishers.com
Info@thecornerstonepublishers.com

Printed in the United States of America.

Paperback ISBN: 978-1-952098-99-4
eBook ISBN: 978-1-957809-00-7

All rights reserved. No part of this publication may be reproduced, stored in a retrieval system, or transmitted in any form or by any means-electronic, mechanical, digital, photocopy, recording, or any other- except for brief quotations embodied in printed reviews or articles, without the prior permission of the author.

To contact the author, please email:
Quannatheauthor@gmail.com

Contents

Acknowledgements v

Introduction 7

Chapter 1 9
   Life's Purpose 9
   I'm stronger 12

Chapter 2 15
   Actions, Inactions and Consequences 15

Chapter 3 21
   Trust God 21
   Spiritual Suicide 24

Chapter 4 27
   Church HHHHHHHUUUUUrrttt 27

Chapter 5 31
   Learning to Speak 31

Chapter 6 37
   Mental Exhaustion and Midnight Hours 37
   The Act of Letting Go 41

Chapter 7 45
   Mom 45

Chapter 8 51
   My Beautiful Princess 51

Chapter 9 57
   God's Grace and Favor 57

- Favor 60
- It's personal 62
- Chapter 10 65
  - Butterflies 65

Acknowledgments

Giving all the glory to my creator. My very best friend and everything else I have always wanted Him to be. God! I wouldn't have made it this far without You.

I thank You for your continued love, grace, and mercy. I thank You for not giving up on me when everyone else did.

To my princess, Jae', I believe God gave you to me to keep me going. I love you so much baby girl. I hope mommy is making you proud.

To my mom, Johnnie Jackson, God bless her soul. I hope you're proud of me and smiling down at me. Thank you for being the best mom that you could be. I miss you so much! I love you forever, pretty lady.

Introduction

In life, I learned that sometimes, we must thank God for the things that He allows us to go through. I wish it were different. I wish I did not experience it. I wish I did not regret it, but I am thankful for the lesson. Growing up, my life was full of fun. Yes, it was not always easy but as a child, I did not know how hard it really was. I did not know what was really going on. However, as I got older, I understood better how life can throw you curve balls. I am out done but very thankful because even though my wings got wet, I still learned how to fly. I hope as you read this book, you learn some new ways to fly also.

Chapter 1

Life's Purpose

As a child, I had the dream to become a nurse but once I went to middle school and realized how many unpleasant things they may see and touch, I quickly changed my mind. I struggled with choosing a career path until my sophomore year in high school. I took childcare classes and part of our classes were to work in the daycare. I learned so much and then realized that it was what I wanted to do. By senior year, I decided I wanted to be a behavior analyst.

However, the schooling on that was longer than I wanted to do. I took a lot of twist and turns attempting to identify my purpose. Still to this day, I struggle with my exact purpose. I do know that it involves working with children, youth, and families. I often am the earpiece for lots of people. It's common for me to meet a person off the street and they tell me their whole life story. I'm also a natural giver, very compassionate and have the heart to help. My prayer constantly is, "Lord, help me be the woman you created me to be." It wasn't until a few years ago when I really started understanding my purpose. I started to realize my journey wasn't just for me. I was equipped to get through it so that I could help somebody else. People didn't just talk to me just because. Instead, they did it because of my God-given talent. There are times when I doubt and question if I'm on the right path regarding my purpose, but God would send me reminders to tell me He is pleased with me and to keep trusting Him. Having a real relationship with God and letting Him be the author of your life is worth it. I'm sure I wouldn't be where I am today without Him. Spend time with God; let Him lead and guide you in the direction of identifying who you are. One of the wrong places to be is to be out of the will of God. Once you understand who you are, then you will identify your purpose. I pray that God gives you clarity over your life and what you have been called to do. Amen

I Learned How Fly in the Rain

I'm stronger

My favorite quote has always been, 'What doesn't kill me makes me stronger.' I strongly believe that since I didn't die from it, I'm now strong because of it. I always thought I was too young to go through all of it but now I have a story to tell. I pray my story helps someone. My test was necessary to me now. What I went through was necessary. They were the basic requirements for my next level. It was all part of my training ground to propel me to my next destination. Let's think about it like math classes. You start from prealgebra, then you can't go to algebra until you understand prealgebra. Then there's geometry and calculus and so on. You can't skip a step without passing the requirements of the first class or you would be lost. When God gives lets challenges come our way, it's to test us and learn from it. When we successfully pass, we move on to our next level. The more you go through, the more you grow. The more lessons you are taught, the more you learn. Your struggles really do make you stronger. Strong people are made from defeating tough situations.

Chapter 2
Actions, Inactions and Consequences

Every action has a consequence. Whether negative or positive, there will be a consequence for everything you do or don't do. In my life, I've dealt with so many different things. As I write today, tears are flowing. I decided to be transparent, in efforts to help someone else. I've endured some hectic moments that I'm surprised that I haven't lost my mind. The moment I became depressed, I tried to fight and overcome it because I didn't want to believe it had become a part of me. I don't trust a lot of people so I had only a few people I would speak to about my problems. For a long time, I refused to believe that depression was even my problem. I refused to accept any form of mental illness but all the while, depression was kicking my behind and had me about to lose my mind. Almost every night, I laid in the bed crying my eyes out before I fell asleep. I would just pray and cry all night. Sometimes, I found myself laughing and crying because I so badly wanted to be strong. I so badly wanted to defeat this and didn't want to accept that this was my life. I would often encourage myself by saying, "Girl, you got this. Stop it." I was in a bad place, and I couldn't understand why it had to be me. It started to get so bad that it became very difficult to get out of bed.

Sometimes when I did, I would be on my way to work then begin to feel that pain and turn around to go home. I didn't know what depression felt like until I experienced it. I felt it right in my chest, like someone was stabbing me. Sometimes, it felt like I couldn't breathe. I wanted to die because I felt death would be a better feeling, a better escape. I tried to sleep my life away sometimes so to not feel this pain or face my reality. I would also ride in my car only to sit in it for hours, crying my eyes out because of the pain I felt. After months of experiencing this awful feeling, I concluded that I needed help. I went to see someone. As I filled out the paperwork, I realized I felt almost every option on the paper except

'Suicide & Murdering someone else.' I remember asking myself, "Is this really my life?"

As I sat and discussed with the therapist, she dug up things I realized were hidden. At the end of the session, I felt worse than I did before it started. I sat in the parking lot and cried my eyes out. I felt useless and unloved. I felt there was no point for me to live anymore. I told God that if He wanted to end me, I was okay with that. I knew my little baby needed me and I never wanted her to feel how I felt. I knew she deserved better than I offered. I was a messed-up individual, and I was only dragging her alone with my foolishness. As time went on, I continued to fight and pray for a breakthrough!! I began to reach out to trusted friends, just to ask them to pray for me. I knew I was losing hope. I needed help fast! I desperately wanted life to get better. It wasn't that it was bad, I was just in a very bad place emotionally. So, because I had a hard time shaking that, it controlled me. The decisions I made only worsened things for me. It wasn't that I wasn't fighting, because every day, I tried! It was just hard!! It's sad to say I allowed depression to control me. Fast forward to now, I'm still fighting! I'm just attempting to fight with a different approach. The space I'm in now, I realize that if I don't keep fighting, I will continue to make matters worse. I was reminded the other day that every action has a consequence. If I don't push myself then I won't ever get out. If I allow depression to get the best of me, then I may lose my life. I had to get motivated to win! I must speak it and believe it! That's the only way I can defeat the enemy that is so badly trying to kill me. I must remember whom I am, and that God has me. My daughter really needs me so no matter how bad I want to; I can't give up the fight. My actions and inactions have consequences. I wrote this to encourage someone else that we must keep fighting. Despite all adversities, we must keep fighting!! It's hard I know, but if we don't, we only aggravate. Someone is depending on us!! Also, in due time, we will win.

Chapter 3

Trust God

I truly thank God for growth and restoration. There were times I probably would have, should have, could have lost my mind. The enemy was so busy trying to get to me. But I pressed on until I started to see God's promises manifesting. What the devil meant for bad turned around for my good. Now I have even a bigger and better testimony of how God rescued me once again. Is my life perfect? Not at all, I still have problems and the devil is still meddling. But now, I have realized my power! The devil only wins when I give up the fight and allow him to. I will not allow the devil, even for a minute, to take control over my life. All that has been spoken against me and meant to take me out has made me stronger.

Sometimes, we hold ourselves back from so much because we don't believe in ourselves or God. God has already paved the way for us to be who He called us to be. We just have a hard time trusting His plan. No one ever said that God's way would be easy, but they did say that it would be worth it. I've always been strong, but I never realized how strong I was until being strong became my only option. I never knew how powerful I could be until I tapped into my inner self. We must stop holding ourselves back and stand on God's word that He has already equipped us with to fight and survive. We tend to trust other people and things before we trust God. What if we trusted God as much as we trust the bench when we sit or the food we buy to eat? We don't know if the bench will fall but we still take a risk and sit, trusting that it will hold us up. We go out and buy different foods from restaurants, trusting it was made right and with love, not knowing if it's going to make us sick, but we still trust and eat it.

Crazy thing is God has never failed us and will never fail us but we still have a hard time trusting Him. Over the years, I've learned so much about God, myself, trust and faith. I can go on and on to explain but I will stop here and leave you with this; as much as you trust to see tomorrow or the next minute, trust God! He's got you! I'm a living witness.

Spiritual Suicide

Ever been in a very confusing place spiritually? Like, you know there's a God. You trust Him, you believe in Him, but you're just so mad at Him it's hard to like Him? You feel so bad because you grew up very religious, but you are really struggling with believing. Yeah, I've been there. It was when God was all I had to call on, but I was too upset with Him to call on Him. I blamed Him in my mind for what I was dealing with. However, I was too embarrassed to voice out in public. Because, again, I knew better. I was really committing spiritual suicide. I did not want to talk to God even though I knew He was my only help. I still loved Him, but I questioned His love for me. Why did He let me go through so much? I thought He wouldn't put no more on me than I could bear. Why did He have so much faith in me? I didn't want to pray but I knew I needed too. I was really in a hard time in my life. So lost, so confused and just didn't know what to do. I call it spiritual suicide, because who I knew I needed, I struggled to call on. It wasn't until I got tired of running, sitting back to realize that enough was enough and accepting that it was my season of pain, hence I just needed to endure. That blessed me. I had to remember that it was only my 'now' but not my forever. Okay, let me help you; your season of pain is just your 'now,' not your forever. Stay focused and prayerful. Even when you feel like God is not there and He doesn't love you, He does! Don't commit spiritual suicide. He said in His word in Psalm 55:22; "Give your burdens to Him and you would find rest." There's so much rest and peace in doing this. Like I said before, keep fighting because you will win. I speak this now over you and those attached to you; no weapon formed against you shall prosper and even the ones we form against ourselves, you will win.

Chapter 4
Church HHHHHUUUrrttt

Growing up in a church was so much fun. It was a place where I met most of my friends. I loved to sing in the choir and dance on the dance ministry. There was even a time where I was an usher. I loved everything about church. Sundays was one of my favorite days of the week. I learned early about the power of prayer and who God was. My mom made us pray and read the bible daily. Every day, before departing, she would anoint us with oil and make us say, "In Jesus Name," as she anointed our heads and hands. I didn't necessarily get saved until about 16 years old. Not because I didn't want to before then but because I was scared, I would drown at baptism. After finally getting dipped in the water, I realized I was scared for nothing. All my friends were baptized way before me, but now I was officially a part of the Jesus team.

There is something we don't often talk about and that is the fact that the church can hurt us sometimes. Let me just say this; if you are wearing the same shoe, you can get through it. It's hard and it hurts but you can get through. "How?" you may ask. First, stop blaming the church and let that hurt go. Yes, easier said than done, I KNOW but forgiveness is the key. It was when I learned that church people are just that, church people, that I stopped expecting them to be better.

Stop focusing on what they did and who did it but focus more on your healing. Healing does not happen overnight, so it will take time. Be okay with taking time. Yes, the bible advises us to not forsake the assembly but there are a lot of assemblies out there. However, believe you can take time away to get you together. Deal with your hurt and let God heal you. I have been that person sitting in church, struggling to focus because you couldn't get pass the hurt you experienced in the church. I would hear the preacher constantly say, "Get rid of the distractions," but I always wondered when and how that would happen.

The church is one of the only places I have ever seen people take their volunteered positions so seriously. In church is where I learned that people can really be jealous of your gifts. They can also be intimidated by your anointing. You do not fight them with fire, you hand them over to God and let Him work it out. If God anointed and appointed you, then no one can stop you from doing it. However, ecclesiastics does tell us there is a time for everything so also be okay when your season is up. Walk away in love and not in hate. I just want to help you. If you are struggling with church hurt, utilize Matthew 18:14-17, prayer, and God. One thing I do know is He can get you through anything, including Church hurt. Let God do the work and you be healed.

Chapter 5
Learning to Speak

I grew up feeling like I could not talk. It was in the time where a child was to not talk unless talked too. What if the child had something to say? What if the child's silence also meant something? I was being hurt and abused by someone who was supposed to love and protect me. I remember being afraid because no one listened. The hurt grew up with me. I wasn't sure who I was for a while and if I was even enough. I was made to feel like nothing. I was stabbed in the back by people I would sacrifice anything for. Was I enough broken and abused? Absolutely! It was in the moment that I realized my past did not dictate my future that I was able to use my voice. What was taking away from my innocence did not define me. I was misused and not treated with care. That was to never happen again. I was not crazy, just the wrong person was trusted concerning me. There's a popular phrase; "Every dog has its day," so their day will come. They will pay because God do not play about His. Not only am I and was I God's child, but I was also a minor. I did not deserve the cards I was dealt. It taught me never to take a child's voice for granted. If they say it happened to them, investigate it. It is horrible to be called a liar when you are telling the truth. I remember how unloved I felt for weeks because it was my words against theirs and no one believed me. I was a young child, what would I benefit from telling lies? Why would I need to lie? I was going to have to die with my thoughts and feeling about this on the inside. God healed me from something I was too young to know I needed at the time. Now I'm older and wiser. I'm so thankful because even though odds started out against me, I still learned how to fly.

I always heard of families having black sheep. I never actually knew what it meant. So, I looked it up. It is defined as a member of the family that is considered a disgrace. In my family, I'm not sure that we had that. Although most times, I'm sure it felt like we could point out who that was. The interesting thing is I think people will always choose themselves, other than each other. I think our bigger issue was we didn't really know each other. This led to us not understanding each other. When you don't understand people, it's hard to get along with them. When I was younger, I remember family always being around. We saw each other every day when we stayed together in a two-family flat. Then at least once a week when we went to church together. Once church was no longer our meeting place, we only saw each other at sad occasions. I always heard that family is important. However, when it came to my family, it didn't seem like anyone cared. I also always heard family is not only whom you are born to but also the family you create. Let me say this; I have met some great people in my life. There are people I met just a few years ago who I know love me. Do I think my family love me? Yes, absolutely! I just believe they don't know how to love me the way I would like to be loved. Again, they don't know me. Take time to get to know your loved ones. Understand this. I have also learned that family can be toxic. Just because you are family does not mean you have to let them interrupt your peace.

You can love unconditionally from a distance. God has put awesome people in my life to fill the voids of family. Do I wish things were different? Yes! But I had to make up my mind not to miss out on life because people didn't know how to love me correctly. I will pray and take the good with the bad and move on. It's not easy, sometimes, you really wish your story was different. Many times, I would think I never deserved the cards I was dealt. However, like the Royalty I am, I adjusted my crown and lived my life.

Chapter 6

Mental Exhaustion and Midnight Hours

You ever didn't want to live but didn't want to die neither? You just so badly wanted things to get better. You went around everyone acting like you were good while you were dying inside. You wanted to be saved but you couldn't find the words to ask for help. You constantly wondered what would happen if you ended it all but knew that wasn't the answer. Again, you didn't want to die, you were just mentally exhausted from pretending. Your silence, your outbursts, your loudest laughs were all cries for help. However, no one was listening. They were used to you making it happen, used to you being so strong. I remember praying and asking God to heal my heart, my soul and my spirit. I was tired of the way I was, and I just wanted to be healed. I so badly needed a breakthrough. I didn't like who I was now.

My midnights, wheeew, my midnights were horrible. The midnight is when everyone has gone away and are unavailable. It's when you are left with just you and your thoughts. You are tired but sleep just won't come easy. Your mind is telling you all kind of stuff. There were times I would lay in the dark. My spirit would feel okay, but my brain was speaking loudly; you aren't enough, you aren't loved, you will forever be alone. Tears were streaming because even though it wasn't real, it felt like it. I felt so misunderstood. I wished people could read my mind. No one knew the fight I was fighting within. I so badly just wanted to go to sleep. Whew! The midnight hours were something else. The worst part is you don't really know exactly what is going on. You just know you feel weird, and something is off.

But in one of those midnights, God met me in my quiet time. He let me know He was and would always be there. That night, He said to my spirit, "I'm not going to let you die in this." I felt like I was losing it, but God told me He was not going to let me die in my mental exhaustion. It was when I needed to be encouraged the most someone would need me. In encouraging those around me, I found myself giving me what I needed. The bible says in 1st Samuel 30:6, "Now David was greatly distressed, for the people spoke of stoning him, because the soul of all the people was grieved, every man for his sons and his daughters. But David strengthened himself in the LORD his God." Sometimes, when you need someone to encourage you through your storm, the person you need is looking back at you in the mirror. God is no respecter of persons. He doesn't mind using you to bless you. Besides, sometimes, things need to stay between you and God.

Mental exhaustion is real. Trust me when I say this; an idle mind is the devil's workshop. I urge you to use your idle/free time to speak to God and allow Him to speak to you through you.

If you are currently having the same depressing thoughts as I had, if you (or your loved ones) are currently experiencing mental exhaustion in your life this period, I want you to know that God sees you, He hears you.

The Act of Letting Go

I had to really think about a lot of things. I was struggling with anger, and I was cold-hearted. I loved people but hated the ones I felt did me dirty. I had to learn to let that hurt go. I had to learn to love with grace. Boy was it hard. I can't say that I still have quite learned it. However, I've learned to be better. I've learned to love in spite of. I learned to remove myself from draining or trigger situations. Most importantly, I learned to be okay with the ways things are. To not let anger control, me but to control my anger. If my thoughts weren't positive, then my actions wouldn't be either. I had to learn to pray more. I had to learn to not fight my battles but to allow God. For His fight was far more better than mine. My fight could get me jail time or worse. I had to remember that God said in His word that He would make my enemies my footstool. Therefore, I decided to let go and let God.

If you are reading this and you still feel hurt from past betrayals, letdowns, heartbreaks, I want to let you know that your feelings are justified. You have all the right to feel the way you do because truly, you have been hurt. But also, at this point, I urge you to forgive them. I urge you to pick up the lessons taught from those experience but forgive them because when you don't forgive, you add to the heaviness of your burdens. Forgiveness helps you more than it helps those who have wronged you.

Say this short prayer with me:

God, I need you right now. Thank you for being available to call on at any time. Your word says in Psalm 61:2; "From the end of the earth I will cry to You, when my heart is overwhelmed; Lead me to the rock that is higher than I." Lord, tonight, I need You to lead me. I need you to carry my burdens and comfort my heart soul and spirit. Whatever is trying to weigh me down, I ask that You take it away. Lord, I need You right now in these midnight hours. Please hear my prayer, in Jesus Name, Amen!

Chapter 7

Mom

Throughout my childhood, my mother was always my best friend. She was my sole provider and all I knew. One of my main goals was to make her proud and happy. She may have made a lot of mistakes but to me, she was the best mother. I know we went through a lot throughout my childhood. However, I never saw my mama fold. She was so strong and not afraid of anything. No matter what she had to do in life to 'make it,' I saw her do. I know we weren't rich, but I never felt poor. There was nothing my brother and I lacked as children. Life seemed pretty great as a child. Even if it wasn't great, my mom did a good job making us think it was. Until that one day, that one time, and that one season where before I knew it, everything changed. It was no longer our little triangle, but our triangle became a square. Our family of three became a family of four. My mom was now a wife. I was so used to my mom, my brother and I. Now it was my mom, her husband, my brother and I. Once my mom fell in love, everything changed. I then learned early on; I didn't care for change. Change was difficult but it must be done sometimes. So, when it comes, welcome it, it may just be a lesson to learn.

The hardest thing I think I ever had to endure was losing my mom. She died on 5th June, 2019. I mean, my heart was completely broken. The year she died was already a trying year. Few days prior to her death, precisely on 1st June, 2019, I spoke into existence that my next six months would be better than my previous six months. I did this with so much belief that things would turn around for the better in the nearest future, but unfortunately, I lost my mom barely four days later. Devastated cannot describe how I felt at that point. I could not believe the state of my life. My first thought was, what am I going to do now? My mom and I didn't always see eye to eye, but I still loved her. I was so hurt. There's nothing like a mother's love and I knew when she took her last breath, it was over for me. I so badly wanted to be strong, but I struggled. I couldn't believe my mom had left me. She always told me that no matter where she was, she would always be there. She couldn't have meant heaven too. I like to believe she's with me, but realistically, that's not enough. I long for her presence. I still struggle with her death; however, I just strive now to make her proud. I want to see her again. She was a woman like no other. One thing is for certain; she loved God and she wasn't putting no one or nobody before Him. She always talked about heaven so I'm sure she's happy up there. To see her daddy again made her happy, I'm sure. If I could have a do-over, I would just say goodbye this time. I knew my mom was sick. She would often say her time was winding up. I refused to believe her. I prayed so hard that God would just heal her. The day before she died, it was me and her. I couldn't muster up any words. I just stared at her body. Her breathing was fast, and she wouldn't open her eyes. Even through that, she looked so peaceful lying in that hospital bed. My thoughts were like, "Please don't do this," but I couldn't get the words out. I often wonder; if I had begged her to stay, would she have? Would the outcome be different? I know my mother was tired. That doesn't bring me comfort though. We all get tired, but we must keep going. I love my mom so much and miss her even more. If I could have her for just one more day,

I Learned How Fly in the Rain
just one more day... I love you mama FOREVER!!

Chapter 8
My Beautiful Princess

When I was younger, I planned my life. I would be a doctor, married with 5 kids and a fine husband. I planned to practice abstinence and to wait until marriage for sex. Life didn't go that way. I had my first child at 19. I was so embarrassed and not ready to be a mom but I didn't want to fail my child. I wanted to be the best mother I could be. I was in labor for 19 hours. It was so hard and long. My oxygen level was low while giving birth, so I had to wear a mask to give oxygen to my baby. I was so stressed and wanted the baby out of me. I fell asleep praying, asking God for strength. When it was time to push, I woke up in pain with the feeling of something coming out of me. I told my mom I felt like using the restroom. She looked and saw my baby's head. She began yelling for the nurse, asking for help. After one good push, I gave birth to a beautiful baby girl. She was so tiny I was afraid to touch her. For the rest of my life, I have promised to always love her and be the best mom I could be. I love her so much. She became my little mini me. We went through so much in life together. Watching her grow up has been such a beautiful blessing.

I so badly wanted to be the best mother I could be. I did all I could to keep her safe. I still felt like I fell short. I made some horrible mistakes, and I took the one thing I loved the most down with me. I thought to find ways to make it up to her because my baby didn't deserve any of this. It was one challenge after another. It started when I couldn't keep her safe. Then in efforts to achieve safety, I was in a disaster. It was horrible. I felt terrible because this was not how I planned my life. Again, my baby didn't deserve this. My princess was a young child, but she handled everything like a champ. I was so proud of her. I used to think, man I wish I had half the courage and boldness she had. I was embarrassed and didn't know who to trust to help me through these struggles. It was such a time in my life. I felt so defeated but I trusted God was going to see us through. I believed that God knew my heart and He was going to come through. There were some crying days but thank God, this storm didn't last long. Before I knew it, I was praising God for overcoming. This lesson taught me to stay firm in believing that the word of God can never come back void. So now, I'm here to tell you to stay firm. No matter what you face, you can overcome. There's a rainbow after every storm so keep believing, keep flying.

I never planned on being a single mother. However, since that was my story, I did what needed to be done. My daughter means so much to me. I knew I had to succeed because my mini me was watching me. I don't tell her all my secrets, but she's really my best friend. We went through so many highs and lows together. I hate some of the things she had to go through with me, but it made me stronger. I introduced my daughter to God at a young age. She was like 3 years old, standing on chair, singing in church. Our pastor used to love to hear her sing. Funny thing is, as bad as I wanted it to be, singing wasn't baby girl's strong suit. Dancing was. She used to do little dances at the church throughout the year. She was on a dance team that discovered her talent. It wasn't until my mom died that we realized how good she really was. She danced at her funeral and blew everyone away. From that moment, she created her name and has been dancing since. I still try every day to be the best mom I can be to my baby girl. Parenting is hard and I would never be able to get as far as I've gotten without God. I just want to encourage you if you find yourself being a single parent. Depend on God for everything. I promise you I wouldn't have made it this far without Him. He's just been a good, good father to the both of us. He actually loves my daughter more than I do. He also can go where I can't to protect her. I'm so grateful to have God in our lives. I may be a single mother, but my daughter doesn't lack anything. It's not because I'm the best mom, but it's because we serve the best, blessed God.

Chapter 9
God's Grace and Favor

After I loss my mom. I was at a very low point in my life. I was so depressed. I lost everything and felt like I had nobody. I couldn't pray and I lost my faith. Everything was going wrong. I was living from place to place. I really wanted to just give up. I've dealt with depression before but this one was on a whole different level. My mom was gone & so was my will to live. I was in a much darker place than before. Before, I knew who to call on and would. This time, I knew who to call on but couldn't. You ever wanted to call out to Jesus, but you just couldn't? I was so upset with Him. I felt He let me down, so He was the last person I wanted to speak to. The good thing about God is He loves us even when we don't want to be loved. I gave up on Him, but He never gave up on me. I still would feel His presence even when I wasn't trying to invite Him in. He blessed me with grace and mercy even when I didn't deserve it. He kept me even when I didn't want to be kept. He loved me in spite of me.

I lost everything, but I was never without my needs. God showed me so much in that season of my life. That season of my life humbled me. I got to know God in a whole different way. I always heard about all the different things that God can and will be. It was now not any longer about what I heard but about what I watched him to be.

Everything I needed, the great I am kept providing for me. At my lowest, God was still there. I learned that God never failed me. God never let me down. He knew what He was doing all along. You may be dealing with some hardships in your life. I pray that God shows up in your life the way He did for me.

Short Prayer:

Lord, whatever the person reading this is dealing with, I pray You have mercy like You did me. I pray You give the grace You gave me. I pray You show up in their lives. Whatever they need, I pray You provide. God, you are awesome, and we love You for just that. Thank for your many blessings. Amen

Favor

One of the best things to have in life is favor from God. It's better than money. When man says no, the Favor of God always is a yes. God's favor is more precious than anything. Favor has gotten me so far in life. Many would ask how I achieved so many things, but I was telling them it wasn't by my doing but God's favor. Favor gave me nice cars, the homes I wanted and jobs I applied for. My mom used to always say favor isn't fair, but it sure feels good. When I was younger, I didn't quite understand. As I got older and experienced favor for myself, I was like, okay, I like this. I believe in favor just as much as I believe in God. I once applied for a house I really liked, it was exactly what I prayed for. One time, the property owner really didn't want to rent it out to me. She felt like I was a wild child and thought I wouldn't be the best candidate. One day, while we were doing paperwork, she said, "I really don't want to rent to you but for some reason, I can't tell you no." I knew it was favor. She couldn't say no because God's favor over my life was taking care of me. I'm so glad God saw fit to favor me. Again, when you are a favorite to God, no one can stop you. Favor has been my portion for a long time.

Short Prayer:

Thank you God for favor. May You bless the person that's reading this with unlimited favor.

It's personal

You had to walk a day in my shoes to understand my praise. While praising, I would wave my hands because I connected to God's goodness. It was the prayers I forgot to pray receiving answers. Somethings I would only think about, I would watch becoming manifested. God really knew what I needed before I even knew them. I never lacked anything. My praise was personal. I gave up religion and gained relationship. God was and is my everything. In the good and the bad times, I knew to praise. Praise was the way I said thanks for what He had done and what He was going to do. Praise was my weapon. I praised Him through songs the most. In the hardest times of my life, I would sing my way through. When I couldn't sing, I would listen to my music and worship. My praise was personal. I had to praise God for being just who is He. Praise and worship brought me through some tough times in my life. If you are ever feeling down and out, turn on some good worship music. Make your praise personal. Allow God to minister to your heart, your mind and your spirit. During praise and worship, chains begin to break, and demons begin to tremble.

The book of Acts 16:25-26 says, "But at midnight, Paul and Silas were praying and singing hymns to God, and the prisoners were listening to them. Suddenly, there was a great earthquake, so the foundations of the prison were shaken; and immediately, all the doors were opened and everyone's chains were loosed." This confirms that when our praises go up, God's blessings come down. The devil has no authority over you when you praise God. So, whatever it is you may be going through now, PRAISE YOUR WAY THROUGH IT!! You got this.

Chapter 10

Butterflies

Sometimes, life throws real big curve balls and I've now learned to not let them affect me. The way you look at situations is what causes your reactions. I used to be the one whom would throw the self-pity parties, but one day, I woke up and realized that I would definitely die young if I didn't change the way I reacted to certain trials in my life. I've always been a firm believer in faith. At first, it was because of what my mama, grandma and aunties told me, but as I got older and experienced my own trials, I started believing on my own. I always thought it was amazing to pray for things and watch them manifest. God is just so good!! My whole life has been a testimony and every time I look over the things I've already overcome, I'm still amazed because it could have only been God. Before the caterpillar can become the butterfly, the caterpillar has to experience being small and not wanted. Nobody is out looking for a caterpillar and describing it as beautiful per say. Despite all, the caterpillar doesn't give up, but keeps its eyes on the prize of one day becoming a beautiful butterfly, that one day, everyone will admire it. If the caterpillar doesn't stay focus and lets the world get them down, then the caterpillar would die and never get to see its better days, restoration and beauty.

In our own world, we must have the mindset of the caterpillar that despite what our situation looks like, we have to stay focused and to keep going. We may have to shut down and hibernate but do it with God in prayer and fasting. At this stage, we can call it the chrysalis or pupa stage, where it's dark cold and the caterpillar is no longer eating or sleeping but waiting to become this beautiful butterfly. In this phase, the caterpillar is allowing itself to mature and to grow to be able to live in its better butterfly days. The caterpillar is now learning perseverance. This is the last step before the caterpillar is free, so that tells us that when we are going through our trials and tribulations, and it just seems like the road has gotten rough and tough, that we are almost there. The harder the battle, the bigger the blessing and breakthrough. The devil never wins, we just sometimes give up too quickly. Also, in these times, we really need to remember Jesus and the promises that He made. Our life experiences are to help us grow and become all that God wants us to be. God does things for Him to get the glory. As we go through, we grow through. Get a caterpillar mindset but don't stay there; stay focused and become the beautiful butterfly God has called you to be. It's not easy but it is worth it.

I'm a firm believer that there is power in the tongue. Also, what you put